THE PUNISHMENT

Tristram,

Please enjoy my words...

J Prichard

2020

THE PUNISHMENT

JOSEPH DANDURAND

NIGHTWOOD EDITIONS

2022

Nightwood Editions
P.O. Box 1779
Gibsons, BC VON 1V0
Canada
www.nightwoodeditions.com

COVER DESIGN: Carleton Wilson
COVER ART: Elinor Atkins (Miməwqθelət)
TYPOGRAPHY: Carleton Wilson

Nightwood Editions acknowledges the support of the Canada Council for the Arts, the
Government of Canada, and the Province of British Columbia through the BC Arts Council.

This book has been produced on 100% post-consumer recycled, ancient-forest-free paper,
processed chlorine-free and printed with vegetable-based dyes.

Printed and bound in Canada.

LIBRARY AND ARCHIVES CANADA CATALOGUING IN PUBLICATION

Title: The punishment / Joseph Dandurand.
Names: Dandurand, Joseph A., author.
Description: Poems.
Identifiers: Canadiana (print) 20220252416 | Canadiana (ebook) 20220252459 |
ISBN 9780889714328 (softcover) | ISBN 9780889714335 (EPUB)
Classification: LCC PS8557.A523 P86 2022 | DDC C811/.54—dc23

Contents

‹‹ | ››

◄◄ II ►►

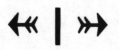

The Unhappy Daybreak

Forever in debt to the last who were sent away
They are still here among us, little and broken
They have the scars of a time when hitting was the thing to do
They are tormented by hands that come at them and penetrate
My mom is one of them and now her brain has decided to fade
She still cries when I ask her about her time there
She can feel the cold hands of that sick priest
She can feel the slaps from the sisters wearing wooden crosses
With each stroke of the strap they smile, glorious and happy
Decades later our elders sit and listen to an apology
Counting the dollars given in one hand, a sort of thank you for surviving it
My mom throws her money into the fire, remembering the cold hands

The Punishment

They took my mom at age five,
put her on a train to St. Mary's,
named after a biblical working girl,
one of the missing and murdered
of the time then and of the time now.

For speaking her own language
Mom was made to work in the kitchen.
For bedwetting, she was made
to wear her soiled sheets all day.
For talking to others, she was made to
kneel for half an hour on the cold ground.
When she broke a glass, she was given
three lashes in front of the whole school.

Through all this she no longer wept.
She became tough, lost her Indian,
was saved by Christ. Years later her son
sits in a madhouse. He is looking for his spirit
but it left a long time ago. When he is asked
in a nice way, he shares his words of madness,
how his mom was not really a mom,
did not know how to be a mom.
She knew, remembered how to punish
and he learned how to be punished.

Today she is one of our elders,
respected for her suffering.
I too have grown up.
I hold a ceremony, a naming ceremony.

I give Mom her Indian name Tsa'Kwi'Ah
which she shares with my middle daughter.
It means *She who remembers.*
And she does; she remembers the punishment—
and we all are punished in her memory,
even if we are told to kneel and forgive the past.

But the past is all we have and in it
we suffer the punishment of a book
filled with the father, the son
and the ghosts of who we are not.

It Was Impossible to Forgive Them

They were lined up and asked who had pissed their beds. The little ones stepped forward, the older ones knowing not to admit anything to the big ugly sisters in their drab gowns of the Lord. The little ones were punished and were not given any food for the day, not allowed to drink tea or water. They went to bed empty and the next morning the sisters asked who had wet the bed. Not one of them stepped forward and this pleased the ugly sisters of the Lord. They were all fed and sent to mass and there they sat. Then they kneeled and then they stood and then they repeated the word *Amen* and the fat ugly father was pleased. The little ones sat back down and they peed their pants and dresses and the father never knew who it was as they all left out the one door to the chapel and ran into the yard and there they played and laughed at the fat ugly father who would later mop up the pee and not say a word to the ugly sisters. He was a good man until night came, taking one boy at a time to molest in the bathroom. Years later all these boys would drink whisky and die in the city one by one. That fat father lived to be eighty and when he met his Lord, God forgave him his sins. The sisters too were evil and they punished the children of God and when they met their maker he too forgave them.

An old priest sits at the bar and drinks vodka and water. He comes there every day and the crowd likes him. They feel safe and closer to God and the music plays and it is a tune about glory and perfection and the old priest gets up and asks a lady to dance and she is honoured and swings with the priest, the crowd cheering them on, and soon the priest kisses the lady and she is under his spell and they go home together and the priest fucks her from behind and crosses himself and the lady smiles and is honoured. When he is done he tells her to leave and then kneels in the corner wanting forgiveness for his sins and gets up to light a cigarette and open a warm bottle of vodka and drink the whole bottle and then there is a knock at the door. He opens it and a young man from upriver enters. The priest is so drunk and satisfied he does not notice the knife in the young man's hand. He tells him to sit and offers him a drink and the young man says nothing because he has come to end the priest for what he had done to him years before in the bathroom of a dark school on an island and the priest takes one last sip of vodka and takes one last drag of his smoke and he turns and faces his maker and the young man slides the knife into his heart and the priest takes a few moments to bleed out, enough time to ask why and the young man kicks him in the face and beats the priest as the blood drains on the floor and the priest dies with his eyes open and his hands clasped in prayer and the young man from upriver wipes the blade off and closes the door.

A Kwantlen boy was sent to St. Mary's when he was five and he was fast and could run forever as this is who the Kwantlen were: they were the tireless runners. The boy was beaten on his first day because he had spoken a word in his language and the church does not want words of savages spoken at this school so he was given three lashes and was bleeding and tried to run but they caught him and pulled down his pants in front of the whole school. He was given three lashes and was bleeding but he knew he would get out of there the first chance he could get and that day came when the whole school was outside watching a play about Easter and the death of Christ and how he rose up and when they nailed Christ to the cross the young boy ran for the river and everyone saw and the sisters and the brothers gave chase and they almost had him but he was Kwantlen and too fast and jumped in and swam downriver. Still they ran after him but he was gone and swam all the way home to the main Kwantlen village where he came to the shore for his mother to take him in. When the church people came to the village he was kept hidden with all the other children and he grew into a great Kwantlen man and is still here today and can still run as fast as any god or devil.

Even the Promise of Freedom

When I was a small boy
I fell on my head.
They said I would be okay
and today I wonder if they were right.

What if I was not okay
and the years later
were all in vain?

What if I could never
be healed and be normal,
and if the girls I loved
really could not see
how much I loved them?

The loneliness: Was that
a part of the show
or was it a given?

The drunkenness and drugs
and abuse and dreams—
the dreams I could never remember
so I slept alone in a bed of thorns
and snakes and demons.
And the loss, always the loss
of a lover who'd found someone
else who had not fallen.
So the little boy is still a little boy
with his scars and knocks;
his eyes are still beautiful

and the girls are now women.
They love his eyes and his words
and they come to him.
They tell him their lives
and he listens and nods.
He nods his broken head;
the soft part where he fell
is of no use to anyone.
He cannot dream
and dreams are needed.

I was in school after kicking
drugs and booze and I was awake
so I took a writing course
and my mind exploded
with stories of woe. Even now
the tales are of loss and forgiveness
and they fill the room.
I walked out a man of words
and they took me in—
the artists and poets and lovers.

They kept me but I needed to go west—
so I got in my car and aimed for the hills.
The west coast welcomed me home
and here I am by the river
where the water is dirty and flows
high. It creeps over the edge
and there is word of flood
but not this year and not next year,
perhaps later when the moon stands
and speaks to us. It is not happy

and tells us this. The moon has
seen it all and with that comes
some wisdom so we listen and learn
and bow our heads not in prayer
but in shame for the world
we have created, a world
we've used and abused
without worry. But the river rises
dirty and the moon watches us—
the ones who did not deserve
such paradise. With our false gods
we conquer the need to fix it
and fixing it is what is needed
when the moon speaks.

When I was a small boy
I was sent to Catholic school.
Mom was terrified of Christ
from residential school so she
gave me to God and he took me in.
The first day I fought another boy
who did not like my brown skin.
I guess he wanted me gone
but I stayed and took him and others on—
The sisters beat me with thick straps
and I am sure they enjoyed this,
a punishment given to them
by their Lord. One day we were sitting
listening to gospel and I could not sit
still so a sister came over and stood
on my hand. Her heels were thick
and black and I screamed in pain.

They took me out of there and the words
of God faded. They took me to the priest
and he took me into a bathroom. He told me
to take down my pants. I did what he asked.
Still today I hate bathrooms.
I remember the one window
and the sun shining outside.
The gleams of rays fell into
the bathroom as the devil rose.
They said I had been fighting.
Mother was too far gone to see the truth.

Now in my fifties I feel the loss of me
and in me there is more to lose,
but not to God.

I am punished ...

for being a liar and a cheat and a man
who cared only for himself.
And for yelling and screaming
while the child hid in her room.
And for fighting when the fight was fixed
and for being a lover once too often.
And the words I place on paper and lies
told in all my poems and stories,
and for never saying I am sorry
to those I wronged. And to those I walked by
and did not help and to the lost and missing
who I wished I could have saved
but I was too busy. Sucking the tar
from the tinfoil and smoking the rock
that gave me the want to want more
and to the people I live beside here
on this island I am sorry I did not care
for you and your loss. And to the friends
I buried I am sorry I could not give
you life. All I could do was sing a song or two.
And to the church I am sorry
for what you did to my mom,
and to my mom I am so sorry
I did not know.

I see faces in the dirt and in the trees
and in the water that flows by
my house. These faces are quite different:
some are old and some I do not know.
When I speak to them they do not answer.

So I close my eyes and when I look again
they are still there staring at me.
At big gatherings I can see faces in
the dirt floor: they all have their mouths open
and they are singing their own songs.
When the drums stop, the faces take
a deep breath and blow the dirt
from their mouths. When drums begin
again the faces change: they become
much older, from hundreds of years
before we ever sat and sang our songs.
Those Old Ones open their mouths
as they breathe the dirt of time.
I would like to thank those who have given me
the gift to write and be a storyteller
for my people. I will walk the right way
and not share everything I've seen
and that I've lived, not to be petty, no:
it is just that there are things we cannot share,
there are stories that are *ours*
and do not write in books,
do not give them away.

I will keep writing as I have to
and need to, joining all the pain inside
with the glory of what is good—
what has been good for this poet
who sits here in his misery and glory
as if it ever meant he would succeed.

Part of a Machine

Each of us has been here
before, so we are told.
The Old Ones know best
and are quite happy
to be here again.

I am new to this, here for
the third time. Before this,
I was a sasquatch. I walked
and walked always unseen
alone along the river.

My days were spent high
in the cedar trees looking
down. When I became an old
sasquatch I lived among
the Kwantlen and when
I was born again I found
myself in a school
where they told me
I was a child of God.
Still I could look down
and see it all.

They told me to be quiet
and not speak Sasquatch.
They told me to kneel
and repent, so I knelt
and repented.

When I grew up and left
the school they told me
I was now a saint
so I went home and there
the people were so silent—
they never spoke
about the lost children,
they never spoke.

As I become my fourth life
I've grown wings and I soar
overhead seeing it all
as if I had seen it before.

A healer burns plates
of food and blankets.
She is from downriver
at the mouth from an old village.

They speak the same language
as us and we are family,
we are all family, those of us
who live by the river.
For centuries we loved
each other and survived.

The healer raises her hands
into the air and searches,
she searches for those
on the other side and they come
to her—they come to the fire
where they eat the food

given to them: their favourite plates
of fish and rice and potatoes
and some berries. You can hear them
as they chew and swallow and enjoy.

They sit down and rest
as they have travelled from
way upriver from a canyon
where they all gather and take
the fish. They are old and not
from our time—we love them
just the same. The healer raises
her hands to the air
and the fire smokes.

The plates are all gone and now
the blankets burn for the loved
as the fire goes out
and everyone is gone.
A little boy checks the fire
to make sure it has burned out.
He leaves and walks home—
there he dreams of the Old Ones.
He can hear them chewing,
he can hear them laughing.

A church burns as the children
are all found buried
far into the ground
and they are all still there.

A church bell rings
and the cross on top is broken.
The windows are all painted
with those who are glorified.
Christ sits on the cross
and he is in pain. He begs us,
he begs us for Salvation
and we eat his body,
we drink his blood
as the big book is open
to page 987: there the words
tell of a great flood
and how we survived.

Yes, we the people of the river
survived all this. The church is lit
as a young boy runs away
into the night. He watches
from behind a tree: the flames engulf
the windows painted with saints.
The broken cross falls
to the earth and the church
crumbles. The boy cries.
He knows what went on in there.
He was told to do this,
he was chosen:

our saviour
our father
our son.

Violence

Six a.m. and the piano plays Vivaldi.
The earth cools for the start of a new winter.
The violins enter and destroy the epic dream
as we awake to the sickness of the day
and we all remember a childhood
swept away from us, the loneliness of
being alone and not liked in school,
how the daily fights to survive it
waned on me as my hands hardened
from all the beatings. But I soon learned
and in the end I could read with one
black eye, a broken nose and two broken
knuckles as I threw a punch too high,
catching the fat kid in the skull.
He stumbled and fell and I was blamed
for it all. I took the punishment too:
five smacks of a thick leather strap.
The sister who gave it to me whispered
a prayer under her breath as she almost
climaxed with her duty to rid me of sin.
I did okay after that and was even chosen
to play Joseph in the Christmas play.
My mom sat in the front row and smiled,
even though Joseph in this Christ's birth
was played by a boy with a black eye.

Grade school was different—the violins
hammered home in me a feeling that
I was special. I was liked by the girls
and they played their games while

we boys played our games and sometimes
we would all meet in the deep forest.
The fairy tales of ours would shine
and we ran through the trees
as the violins hammered us
with such grace—once I was caught
by a cute girl with long dark hair
who had been looking at me in class.
She came up to me and kissed
me on the lips, said she liked me,
then ran away. I lost her in the trees,
then another girl found me, older than
all the others. She told me she liked me,
then slipped her tongue into my mouth.
It was paradise as the violins became violent.
She laughed and ran way and I lost her
in the trees too, found myself alone
again tasting both girls on my lips.
When I came out of the forest,
I looked back and saw butterflies
spreading their wings and dancing
to the soft strings of a lone violin.

In high school, I was
a bum a thief a lover a liar.
There were others like me,
and we joined hands to be a gang
from the south side, then joined hands
with the crew from the west side
and sold drugs and drank every weekend.
We fought the east side and fought
the north side—it was glorious.

I became a better fighter but was skinny.
I took a couple good shots to the head
and fell knocked out—wonderful feeling.
Yes, it felt good to fall asleep
for a second or two. When I got up,
you could hear all the girls cheering me on
and in I went, stood my ground,
my crew behind me. But then
the lunch bell sounded and we ended
our war. Yes, the war is over—long live
the fighter, a skinny kid from the south side
who never knew the emptiness of peace.

Sinking In

If ever you see me on the road to nowhere,
stop and ask me any question about life
and I will tell you the same thing I told the priest
when he held me down and told me to pray for mercy.
I will tell you that down here you can see hell,
and you are about to go in if you don't get off me.
He did and repented and instead sinned on other boys.

I tell you this so when you stop me on the road,
you do not think I will be able to give you
the right or wrong answer but will answer the truth
and with truth comes the pain of abuse.
To those who do not believe in me, that is okay too
because I really couldn't care less if you do or don't.
When I walk away, do not stare at me
to turn and tell differently the words
that I have carried on my back since I was five
and the first cold touch of a priest destroyed me
into the man I am today, and I am a man,
not one to choose my words lightly,
so listen and learn a few things about life
and how hard it is for a boy on the floor.

This man took his lighter, had already poured the gas,
had already locked all the doors, then lit it—
and up that old school went in flames and they came
from all the villages to watch it burn
and some even brought their children
and told about all the evil that went with this school
and up it went—the roof fell in and children began

to play around the flames. They laughed and did not know
what was really going on while the man who lit it
was sitting on a hill watching the glory of his task
and feeding the fire pages from the bible, creation to salvation,
the children joining hands and circling the burning school
as the walls fell in leaving only bricks and the cross at the top.
So the man who lit it went up and poured more gas
on the cross and lit it and everyone stopped
and watched as the cross burned and went up into the sky.

Then they went home, the kids sad because they wanted
to smash the bricks, while the man who started it all
sat on the hill, lit a cigarette and smiled as the smoke of abuse
burst once more and the clouds became black and the heavens
opened and down came God—he was happy and touched
the man who lit the fire and the man, bursting into flames
and smiling, crossed himself, thanking God
the father
the son
the fucker who created all this mess.

On our island we have an old church. We plant flowers
and cut the grass and every so often outsiders come
to hold a wedding or maybe a film crew uses it
for a bad TV movie. We drive or walk by and never go in
anymore as the followers are no longer here
but we cut the grass and we wash the stained-glass windows
once in a while and we plant new flowers
and it is the nicest, most well-kept building that we have here.
But no one goes in and if they do, they do not stay long.
Inside there are paintings of all that went on
when this religion took hold of the people

and we were told to kneel and pray,
and told we were savages and God was for us
and we were for God—that seemed like a fair deal
but when God came down and said He had a full house,
we threw our two pairs into the ground
and as we knelt we knew even God cheated at cards,
so we waited until he was drunk on holy wine
and asked him to play a game of dice.
He bet all he owned, which was the universe,
and we rolled two sixes and he said *No fair!*
and turned the church into the church it is now:
empty as the new flowers bloom in their madness.

Hit the Ground Running

We whispered in the classroom
and we were ready to get up and jump
out the windows of this school—
I would have been the first to leap
and fall but the bell was near three
and I was challenged by the school bully
so we met in the front of the school
and he slammed me to the ground—
I got up and he came at me again
but this time I kicked him in the belly
and down he went, I was on top of him,
I slammed my fists into his nose and jaw
and as he lost consciousness I was going
to kill him. The teachers pulled me off,
and sent me home where my old man
waited with his thick black belt—
this was not the first time he beat me
but now I was older and near a window
so jumped out and floated in the air so free
and when I hit the ground I was already running,
the old man so surprised kept swinging
but I was gone, never went back,
and have been running ever since.

The Heroic Episodes of Desire

I have tried God and I have tried the Devil both were not a success
they both had some good stories but in the end they were both hell
they tried to hammer me into a good saint when I was a child
I forgave more than I deserved and the beatings were the same
if God hit me then the Devil would help me and I would pray
they told me to pray so I prayed but I prayed to the Devil
he did not answer nor did God he just sat there on an altar
later when I was on the streets I looked for them both
in a soup line a man speaks the word of God but I do not say amen
I get my soup and sit in the corner with the other drunks
we sip our soup and sip our sour coffee and we listen
after we are told to leave as there are no more beds
we all walk out to the streets and we each go to our beds of sand
God watches us as we piss our pants and we sleep in our wetness
as the morning comes I am still here and I am still a drunk
the cross around my neck dangles and swings
as I puke the night of cheap cooking wine onto the sidewalk
I look up to heaven but heaven is gone as the gates of hell open.

Candles

Questions and answers and more questions
of why there are those who take our girls downtown.
The prayers and candles burned as we sang songs
and asked for them back but they never gave them back.
Usually when we do find them, they are already gone,
those who had taken them having slipped back into their holes
to sit and wait for the next girl to stumble by and take
and cut into pieces and spread around the world.
When we did find them, they were not whole,
no they were in pieces and we put them back together
and lit more candles and we sang more songs
as those who took them hid in their holes.
What the answer to this one is, no one knows
as the candles burn.

When they found him kneeling in the corner, he was wearing
his best frock and they took him to the sacred ground of their church.
They laid him to rest as if he deserved this—and he did,
but so did the boys he ripped up when he was taking care of them.
They trusted him because God said so and when God speaks
you listen, or so the story goes, but this man liked young boys.
He took them to his room late at night while the others slept
dreaming of their homes and their mothers. They did not hear
the screams of the boy who had been chosen because the priest
liked his eyes. He told the boy to open his eyes and the boy screamed.
Later in life when he was older and back home, he threw the rope
up to the hanging tree and stepped away. He no longer screamed
but the priest was kneeling in the corner—he was to be taken
the next day to face charges of rape but he could not face God
as his wrists dripped, as his eyes looked for the eyes of the boy

but the boy swung side to side and the blood of the priest
was not the blood of God, or so God said.

They met on the corner of Main and Hastings
and soon loved each other and loved the blackness
of their favourite drug. When they awoke each day,
they walked the streets looking to steal and what they stole
they traded for heroin and then they would tuck into an alley
to cook the medicine and put it in a needle they shared.
And as the drug took them, they sat down while others walked
by and never even noticed them there, their eyes open
and mouths open, breathing. The drug destroyed more and more
of them: they used to be so young and beautiful
but now they rested and aged and died a little more
each time they fixed themselves. When they got up
to chase more of the drug, they got a room and shut the door
and cooked their supper of poison; when the needle was ready,
they shared it and sat there with their eyes open and mouths open
as the world outside this room walked by as if they never existed
but they did not, no, as they faded into a needle.

Shaking the Tree of Memory

The shadows fall where there used to be someone—
Sirens can be heard in the distance, but are getting closer
and closer to where the shadows were; now all that is left
is the memory of someone. The sirens stop
and the bulk on the sidewalk is lifted into the ambulance,
but it is too late: they try and try to restart the heart
but all they can hear is shadow and the street becomes
quiet as the other shadows are not ready to be taken away,
so slip into the edges to drive needles into their arms,
to become the glowing addicts who have had way too many
chances. But one day they will hear the sirens
as they come around the corner and into the edges.

At a big gathering downriver from here, the doors opened
and the people came in and sat down in their groups
and the songs began and the fires, there were three of them,
were going hot and the dust mixed with the smoke
and your eyes watered but you kept singing loudly
as did all the other people who had travelled here to witness
the work by the family who were remembering a loved one.
Then the tables of food came out and one group sang
a dinner song. The elders were fed first and then the rest
and then young men came and took away the tables
and the family began their work: they called witnesses
and money was given to those who would help
and then the work began. When it was over,
the family gave all that they had away to their guests
and then the guests left and the family left,
and the fires went out and the room was cold
as the spirits began their own dance.

Had the worst day of fishing in years—everything went
wrong. It started with the boat not getting enough fuel
as the tank had water in it so I floated past our village
and waited for the engine to start and it did, so I went slowly
around our island and up to the eagle's nest
and threw out the net but it went out wrong.
I had to fix it as it had gone over itself
and was not fishing right, then I was too close to shore
and the net snagged so I put the motor to full reverse
to try to pull the net off the snag and it finally snapped.
When I pulled it in, it had been torn in three places
so I joined the pieces back together then went up again
and threw it out properly this time. A fish hit, so I went over
and pulled the net up and up, and there was the fish
but not properly snagged in the net—and as I pulled up
the net the fish fell out and back to the river
so I let the net go and drifted some more.
The net snagged again and this time it would not break,
and I pulled it hard and it finally gave way.
When I pulled it in, half of it was gone so I decided to quit
and when I was pulling my boat up to the trailer
the wind was blowing hard and I could not get the boat
on the trailer properly, it took me half an hour
and I was soaked, my boots were full of water
when I got in my truck and pulled my boat up
and went home and unhooked the boat from my truck
and there to meet me was my dog who looked at me
and turned and never said a word to me.

The New Haircut

I met a man on the streets wearing a crown
of thorns, pants that were too long, shirt
ripped with holes in all the right places,
places where a sword had slipped in—
He was not bleeding, he told me, because
they'd drank all his blood and eaten his body
at the mission soup kitchen, so I told him
he looked pretty good. He said he'd just
come down from the cross and his hands
and feet hurt from the spikes they'd driven
into him and he was quite thirsty, so I gave him
some wine and he said *Thank you* then was gone
up the street. I did not see him for three days
and when he appeared he was not the man
I'd met before; he told me he'd been saved
and the mission had given him new clothes
and a haircut and now he did not look like
he belonged here, told me he was going home,
gave me a piece of bread and told me to forgive him.
And I did—I forgave him for all his sins.

Last Stop

A medicine woman came to the last house on the street.
She was gifted with tea and tobacco and smiled
and the child who was sick was brought to her.
She cradled the child in her arms and blew upon
the child who went to sleep after days of fever
and then the child was healed and the healer said goodbye
and went to the next house and again it was a sick child.
She blew on the child and the child was healed—
the healer thanked them for the gift of a blanket
and some smoked fish and she was on to the next house
where she came upon an old friend who was barely able
to breathe, so she blew upon him and inhaled his sickness
and blew it outside into the air. The man went to sleep
one more time—he was at peace and the healer smiled
and walked out the door. There were no more houses left
but there was a drunk man curled up at the door
of the old church so the healer went up to him
but there was nothing she could do. She sat
down with the man and began an old song
and the words hit the air as her brother passed.

The Hunting Grounds

The rabbits run and the cat watches them from underneath my boat
waiting for the right moment to attack, waiting. The young rabbits
do not know danger and when they come close to her she attacks,
has a young one by the throat and it screams, then when I get up
and go outside for a smoke all I can see is a tail, fur everywhere;
the rabbits are gone to bed, the cat is asleep and I pet her, she purrs
dreaming of river rats and snakes and small birds—
this is her hunting ground and she is the queen of the dirt.
I finish my smoke and go back to bed and close my eyes:
my dreams are not of river rats and snakes, no, I dream of her,
the last lover, as she takes off her clothes and comes to me.
We entangle and untangle and we enter the other and she is love,
the love I used to have when I was half a man—I was kind
and listened, I was gentle and rough and she liked that;
I would take her to where she wanted to be.
She left me for another man and it is like that in this day
so I am alone in my bed as the rats and snakes are so divine.

Seconds to Centuries

I watch the seconds tick away and am aware of
each one; the clock on the wall has been there
since time first came to me. Now the spiderwebs
fall from the clock as another second falls ...
I sip a hot cup of coffee, light a smoke and sit
by myself. The kids and the dogs and the cat sleep
this warm Monday. We have been in this house
for twenty-three years and the seconds fall.
I came home to where my mom was born
in 1942. She is still here but her mind left
a year ago. She dresses as if the winter is
blowing but it is a hot summer. She remembers
residential school as if she has just returned—
those memories never leave even if her mind
has left her. She tells me stories I have heard
a hundred times before. I remind her and ask her
questions and she begins to cry. She knows
the answers but cannot find the words.
She asks for a blanket so I get her one.
As the room flames we talk some more
and then she falls asleep. I go to my home
where I have been for twenty-three years.
The clock on the wall is tangled
with spiderwebs—the seconds tick away
as the memories are welcomed home.

1827 when the fort is built beside our village.
They are all men with long beards smoking pipes.
We go there and they tell us to leave
so we leave and watch them build the fort.

We offer them help. They tell us to leave.
So we leave in our dugout canoes
paddling home watching the fort
burn to the ground. One of our men
was unhappy being told to leave
so lit the walls and the men with beards
ran to the river trying to save their walls
as the flames overcame the night.
This time we did not offer to help.

1828 when they move right across the river
from us. They welcome us but we do not go
as the walls still smell like smoke. We tried
to light this one too but they were ready—
they had buckets of water to put out the flames.
We watched them from our village and still
they welcomed us. We do not go to the fort
today as they fire their cannon our way
just like they did in 1829.

The trains still go past our village and head east
or west, the same train my mom was put on
when she was five, her mother scolding her
for crying, her older brother taking her hand.
They got on that train and she was never the same—
she has the scars, they punished her abused her
completed her. She now is frail and broken
and she still remembers that train slowly leaving
the station across from the fort, the smoke rising
up, the train heading west. She got on a boat—
the ocean was the road. They got off the boat
and walked an hour uphill. There in the distance

you could see the giant cross, Jesus nailed to it.
The children were all wet and cold. They cried
for their mothers but no one would ever hear them.
Even sixty-five years later my mom still cries.
She has a cross on the wall but Jesus is not
bleeding. His eyes are half-open and he stares
at her as she weeps. She looks at where
her hands were broken by the sisters,
her bent fingers. In the distance
the sound of a rumbling train—
she can hear it from her small home.
The train whistles
as the scars are healed
and the child she once was
appears again
as the train heads west.

The Familiar Scent

I burn some old medicine and the scent is wonderful—
it fills the room I sit in every morning before the day begins.
The scent crawls upon me and I think to myself
that it will all be okay in the end when I take that final scent
with me over to the other side where those who went before
me are waiting so patiently for us to come
as those before them also waited for them to bring their scents.
And when you get there, all the smells of your past
come to you only and the others know this and smile—
they try to remember their scent but it has left
so now they breathe in the same air over
and over as they wait so patiently.

My empire of filth is carried to the street
where I have taken up residence and my neighbour
is an old cat with only one ear and a face so tragic
you can tell he has been in many scraps
here on this street where he is king. Those who know him
or have fought him keep their distance and he comes up
to me each day and brushes up against me as he knows
I am like him, king of this street with only one ear
and I have only one eye as the other eye was lost
in a knife fight with an old drunk who was good
with the blade, but I took his heart and the crowd cheered
for me and I swear they yelled *Long live the king!*
but I could have been wrong as I could not hear
with one ear and one eye gone. The cat goes up
the street as a new boy has showed up and wants this territory
so the old cat with one eye and one ear goes at him
and they tangle and tangle and then it is over as fast

as it began and the old cat crawls back to me and dies
in my arms and the new boy does not like me, he never
comes to me as I sit here in the death of a friend
and we both try to listen to the street but cannot.

I will make you hurt if you want me to, but it will hurt—
you will not like it but if you come to me in the shadow
of a half moon when the night spirits have gathered
for the feast of the devil so you invite all the cheaters
and liars you have met in this life and ask them to sit
and watch as I begin the work for you: I light the fire
with my eyes and order in the food for the feast—
it is brought in by black birds who when standing
are eight feet tall and their wings sweep over the floor
of this place we have gathered, and hell opens up
and the fire is lit and I sing a song for you. The cheaters
and liars gorge themselves on overcooked fish and carrots
and rice and lemon pie and when they are done
the black birds sweep in and take out the empty tables,
the leftover bones fall into hell and the fires now burn
as hot as the sun. I stand and tell the gathering
that you will now be changing and so you stand—
I touch you on the head and you disappear into hell,
the fire burning all as you rise up and are now a bear,
you are reborn and everyone sings a song for you.
You dance like a bear around the gathering and then
we all leave, and you are still there as the bear
as hell opens for you and your claws.

The Other Side

They said I was a genius
and my poetry was unlike any other's,
so I wrote and wrote until the day
I knew my heart was going
to stop and then it did stop—
there was that moment of worry
but what did I have to worry about?

There would be nothing left and
you cannot change any of it
after you are gone, in that little window
of here and there I was okay,
it was okay to whimper a bit
and so I went to the other side
where they all were waiting for me,
or so I hoped, but they were not,
they were all the same as me—
having ended up here at the same time.

We were told by a sweet voice
to relax, not to worry anymore
because it no longer mattered.
So we all got in line as if waiting
for a free meal of soup and bread
and the voice spoke again, only to me,
saying I'd lived a good life, I had written
a couple good poems but those poems
no longer mattered, and the voice told me
to kneel because I would be next, so I waited
there on my knees as the others before me

went into the light and never came back
as if they never mattered in the first place.

The Rusty Key

Inside my mind there was an old key
and when I turned it the air flowed
the sound of rust breaking the silence
I could see everything
this happened when I was nine
and had already been abused
the scars were on the other side
of the key and what was in there
if I could count the times I had faced the belt
I would tell you he was angry at me
and I never figured out why
I think he was repeating what his father did to him
if that made it all right then it was all right
I never repeated this with my son
even when he bit my hand
the key is now thrown away
and the rust sleeps
as I became a father I was soon aware
of the hurt inside of me
I never have told anyone about it
not even my kids
they have enough to wonder about
in this hard life we have
so I love them with kindness
and try to not ever raise my voice
this was not always the way for me
I yelled and screamed not at them
but close enough for them to hear me
now I speak as if the key was never there
the sound of the belt

the look in his eyes
repeated and forever rusting.

Ceremony

They would come and sit in the park and share a pipe
nothing holy or sacred no it was a pipe of glass
the tip burnt black and their lips chapped and chipped
their teeth were brown and so too their fingers
they lit that pipe over and over and it burned them
when they'd smoked it all they needed more
and so they danced, danced along the street corner
and men would come to use them, tossing a few dollars.
When they had enough they found the man with the rocks
he would give them small pieces for the few dollars
and go back to that park and the ceremony began
lips chapped and chipped tongues dry they smoked all
they had earned and then went to the dance
they danced like puppets as the glass pipe smoked
and their minds to dust they danced as the street opened
it opened for them and they fell down a hole
where the ceremony started and this time
they all danced as the glass pipe turned to dust.

In the Park in the Middle of the City

She brushes off the sick, inhales their disease.
She lives with them in the east of the city
where they all gather, coming only once a year
to this park in the middle of the city.
One by one they come to her—she takes their pain,
eats it like cake and she spits out the bad parts,
a puddle of pain at her feet. The next one comes,
an addict who has lived far too long for his own good.
She circles him and speaks words of magic,
he begins to tremble and falls to his knees,
she breathes on him then breathes in his poison,
spitting it into the puddle of pain, then touches him.
He stands reborn but the addict in him overcomes
a few hours later—they say he took a hot hit
of a good drug and he died right there on the floor.
Later, the healer was done. She had saved some
but most fell in the hours that followed. You see,
she could not save them from the death they had all along.

The Joke of Consent

The white church is empty and longs for a few songs and prayers
They burn other churches up country and splash red paint on statues
We found some children long forgotten and they said to us, *So what?*
Each child had a heartbeat and a spirit and they need love
We burn plates of food for them and hope this will fill the emptiness
But we know how this ends: in another statue, in another church to be
     burned as the ashes to ashes
When we burned the food a child appeared and was weeping
She told us there were so many of them and some were cold
We burned blankets for them and the girl became flames and ashes
This is another day in who we are and who we once were
The lasting sorrow is our happiness and the other side agrees
The gentle touch of a child's smile opens the fire as we submit

We Came from the Sky

With every day the sun has risen and fallen
and the Kwantlen go to the river where they throw their nets
and the fish hit in the hundreds to be taken home and cleaned
and put away for smoking when the weather cools.

And fifty more suns have risen and fallen
and the Kwantlen start their fires, the smoking of fish on full
but there is a strong wind and the trees are bending.
The fire keeps going out and the fish is not yet fully smoked.

The winds follow the next three suns and then stop
and the fires are going, the fish is smoked and taken down
and the people who have fallen from the sky are happy
to know they have enough fish for the winter.

The next two suns, the snows begin to fall,
the world is white and cold and the winds
can now cut through clothing. The people stay inside
and light their fires, sleeping close to the flames
as sixteen moons fall and rise and then the spring winds
warm the river as the new sun rises one more time.

The Rumours Fly

Into this world we are tossed here and there. Where we land
is where we land, and if I were a betting man, I would have put
down a few dollars on my time being here to be short—
and ending violently. I was close a few times:
I've bled pretty good and if you look closely at my face
you can see the scars of being kicked even when I was already
knocked out cold; when I woke up, I said it was all my fault—
and it was—then I gave just as much as I received.
When they stitched me back together I was reborn;
I am still here where I landed, but I did not ever land
on my feet. No—right on my ass, where I belonged.

End of November and the rains have not stopped
but it is still too warm for winter and we are all confused.
We do not sleep properly, waking every hour and thinking
we have slept all night but really, we only get minutes
here and there and our eyes are tired—we look like
we have not slept at all. Still some of us do our thing
and others do their thing and we get along just fine,
there is no drama here but we sit and wait for it:
usually it shows itself in the form of gossip or rumour,
sometimes there is a death and we, all the living
that is, feel good and bad about this as we feel lucky
it is not us, it is someone else so we stop our bickering
and bury the poor soul and feast on fish and rice
and freshly made pies of apple blueberry.
Of course there is always an apple crumble
which we top with whipped cream as the poor soul
goes up into the air and when they are done,
the feast is done, the rumours fly.

I remember a friend of mine who sold heroin and crack.
He was very good at it and he lived that way until
another man shot him seven times and he fell.
He breathed one more time, then he was gone forever
and we put him away and as he floated up to the sky
we all looked up and cried for him and left the graveyard.
I thought to myself that never in my life had I dug a grave
for anyone, it was always someone else who dug the hole—
but I have *filled* many holes in my time and when we place
the last shovel of dirt on my friend who sold heroin and crack
the rains were still falling and we all left the sacred ground
as the shovel started all over again—
this hole would also be filled by wet dirt,
by the sweat and tears of loved ones
who would also look to the sky.

A Man So Great

1

The church lights were turned on
while the father lit candles.
A man from the village walked in,
kneeled and crossed himself.
The father told the man to sweep the floor
so the man got a broom and swept the floor.
Then a woman entered and crossed herself
as she knelt before the cross and Christ,
so the father told her to wipe down the benches.
Another man entered, did the same,
the father told him to get everything ready
for the service. Then another woman entered,
knelt, the father told her to open the doors.
Then all the people from the village came in
and sat on the hard benches so the father
crossed himself and spoke the words of Christ
and all the people looked down and the father
said some more words and began to sing a hymn
and everyone tried to remember the words
and Christ stared down from his cross
as the door of this hell closed.

2

A man was homeless for some time,
once a great chief of his people at the mouth
of the river where they had been since time began
and others from all parts of the river came
to hear him speak and share his knowledge
but now he sits in a corner where he has finished
his bottle as the world around him struggles
up and down the street and the man snores,
he has pissed his pants, he has puked on his coat—
a woman sees him and remembers he was once
a great man, wakes him up and helps him
and both go stand in line for a coffee, some soup
and some kinds words about God. They go sit
in the park that is full of dirty pigeons and sip
their hot coffee as the birds circle them looking
for some crumbs from the bread of the Lord
but the man opens his bottle, sips as the woman
cries—she knows this will not last, the birds know
this will not last and the man empties his bottle,
gets up and says goodbye to the woman.
Up the street as the birds circle him one more time,
the man falls and dies there on the street
where he was once a great man.

The Healer

Out in the cedar forest a small child played and
chased birds, and when she tired and sat down,
she waited for the first animal to come,
an old wolf limping up and sitting in front of her.
She leaned into his ear and whispered ancient words
then wolf stood up, no longer limping.

Next old owl flew in and sat in front
of the healer and she leaned in and whispered
her ancient words. The owl flew away
as if it was the first time it had taken flight,
free of all the pain it had suffered in its life.

Then an old sasquatch came to the girl.
She whispered ancient words into his ear
and he stood up and grew a foot taller.
He walked slowly away as the healer
stood up and left the cedar forest
whispering ancient words.

In the city, the needles keep our lost
and missing warm; we sing songs for them
as a healer enters the streets
and goes up to each woman and girl
and touches them. They fall to the ground
and are saved, they are found,
their families come and take home
their mother their daughter their sister
to give them a proper ceremony.

And as the smoke of them rises
the street healer walks farther
into the hell of the city
and meets our drunk men.
As she touches each one,
they are saved
they fall
and their loved ones come
to send them to the other side
with such love and grace.

As the smoke rises the street healer
goes deeper and comes across
a young couple huddled beneath
a torn blanket and she touches them—
they rise up into the air and turn into smoke.
As there was no one who loved them,
the healer takes them as her own
and guides them to their peacefulness
hugging each other as the healer
touches herself
and she too goes up
and up
and
up.

Where Were You Last Night?

The drums were so loud and everyone
danced to the beat and went into
a frenzy and the men and the women
screamed to the lust that swept over
all of us and in the end we went home
insane with the culture we had lost
long ago and even now they call us
savages and they tell us to repent
but we just laugh in our own language
and we laugh at the colony that sits
idle and unaware of the revolution
that began twenty winters ago when one
of our own was murdered and left out
in the cold rains of the west coast
and we sat in our boats in protest
of the lack of empathy for our loved
one who was found on a farm just west
of us and there she was fed to pigs and
the man who did all this sits in a warm prison
with three meals and a bible for his thoughts
and when he opens to page three hundred
they tell him he must repent but he never does
and they tell him to read on as lunch is served
and today it is grilled cheese and a tomato soup
with a bit of salt and he sips the cold juice and
he kneels and tries to pray but all the loved ones
he killed appear and they tell him to turn
the page and read on about the Devil
and he does and he likes how this story
goes as he bites into his grilled cheese.

They call us civilized and we look to the west
of us and we throw our nets into the river
as the small fish have come back and it is
a few days into April and we take the nets
home and we shake out the small fish and we fill
up our buckets and we go home and we dip
the small fish into some flour and then place them
in a hot pan that sizzles oil and we cook them
for a few minutes each and then we feast until
our bellies ache and then we look to the east and
there is where the city begins and the streets
are filled with all our brothers and sisters
who have arrived and they line up for a cup
of coffee and some cookies and they walk away
and go back to their one-room shithole
and crank up the heat but the furnace has never
worked so they curl up with some old blankets
and chew on the chewable cookies and sip
the blazing hot cup of shitty coffee and the streets
begin to move and all the dealers and the drunks
and the working kids become devoured by the perverts
and the wicked and they sell their souls for
a five-dollar bill or even less if they appear to be dirty
and most are and the doors of help open
and dregs go there and they beg for existence
but that is never shown to them and they take
down their names and give them a number to call
if they need to die and the revolution rages
and the protestors pound their drums and sing songs
of yesterday and as this pours into the gutters
a young angel of a girl walks down to the corner store
for her grandma and buys a pack of smokes

as her grandma chokes and lights another to burn.
The shelter we surround ourselves with crumbles
and burns in the warm sunlight of this April morning
and our people all gather inside our longhouse
and we light the fires and we cover our hearts
with blankets and we give out quarters
to those who have been invited to witness
the work of the day and today the work
is to remember a loved one and the family cries
tears of memory and then they feast and thank
the cooks and the work begins and each corner
there is song as the work goes on and when it is
all over the family brings out gifts and give all
their possessions away and then the drummers
begin one man's song and he blesses the floor
and when the fires go out a lone boy closes the door
and walks home and as he does the revolution
can be heard coming from the city streets
where the taken and the forgotten have all
gathered and there they hold their own ceremony
as the fires burn in the gutters and this is how
it is and when the city ceremony ends that murderer
closes his big book and he turns off the light and
he puts his head upon his pillow and he dreams
of murder and what he might have for breakfast.

Perhaps the Only Thing

The scent of fire aims itself upon me
We the people rejoice in our ceremony of the afterlife
Children play the bone game and someone cheats
The scent of God is lingering in the winds of shame
They buried all the secrets in the back of the shed
Whispers of death and abuse walk in the door
Cherish the after as the now is upon all of us
Decide if you are perfect or a bit scarred and broken
Challenge the unexpected and the desires of a man
Witness the work by the family who are not alone
Fall into cool waters and come out burning with hope

Keep It for the Endless Nights

Far upriver there were stories about a man
who could control the weather and it is said
he could also control time with ease and loved
that he could control the world which he did
with such malice that the people of the world
decided they would get rid of him. His time
came when he decided to freeze all the waters
and all the people, they too froze and the man
was all alone and died soon after as he too
became frozen from the inside out.

They say a sasquatch came here the other day
looking for a child to have for herself so took
one from a village and the mother of that child
was so stricken with sorrow that she left this
world because she thought her child had also
gone over to the other side but that child lived
with the sasquatch until the sasquatch became old
and the child who was now a woman plunged
a knife into the heart of the sasquatch and watched
her bleed out and then the woman walked back
into her village and learned her mother had died
on the day she'd been taken. The woman sat
by a tree and there plunged the knife
into her own heart as songbirds sang.

Today the hurt is much more hidden but it is there:
we see some of it on the highways and dark alleys
of the city and even see it in our homes but we've
tried to destroy the evil when we can, and we've sent

a few over to the other side to suffer their fate
but still today we hear of our young and how
they can't stand it here so they make the jump
and away they fly to the side where all evil creeps
and false healers and sasquatches who steal children
live again untouched by the grace of those
who truly believe this is a hard life but a good life.

The Shadows of a Cold Day

They looked like every person looked
but there was something different about their eyes
that caused us all to look at them differently
but we did not say much to them and they carried
on to the mountains and there they lived by themselves
and there they became who they were to become.

We would sing songs about them and we always left plates
of fish and would burn the plates every year on the same day
and as the smoke went up into the darkness of a cold day
they would all come down from the mountains
and they would feast on their favourite dish
and all we could see of them through the smoke was their eyes
and we knew it was them and they knew who we were
and they closed their eyes as the fire died
and we all went to our homes on the island
where our dreams were filled with those people
from the mountain and they could look right through us.

One day a great fire claimed the forest below the mountains
and we never ever again saw the special ones
as they had slipped into the fires and the trees burned
and burned into ashes and then the wind blew those ashes
and they covered the island and all the people who lived there
and as the smoke finally cleared all you could see
were the shadows of the special ones.

A lone child walks along the edge of the river
looking for rocks made by our people way back when
the ice had melted and she finds one and places it
with the other rocks she has found, made by our people
into knives and tools that they used as the ice slowly melted
and created this great river that the child walks beside
and as she is about to go home when something flashes
and catches her eye and she bends down and picks it up
and stares at it and realizes that our people did not make this
but it was made by the special ones who lived in the mountains
so she gently throws it into the river and there it falls
to the bottom of the river never to be seen again.

The people on the island invited the people
who lived beside the river to a great gathering—
everyone feasting and dancing and singing old songs.
In the far end of the building an old man stood up
to sing a song no one had ever heard before.
Everyone at the gathering began to cry
and when the old man finished his song
everyone looked at him and had ever seen eyes
like his. As everyone continued to cry
he walked up the mountain never to be seen again.

Just Like a Spirit

In a perfect world there would be meetings between an old spirit
and a young new spirit where they would share words
and the old spirit would give the new one a piece of old cedar
and would make the new one make four promises to keep
throughout their life and the new one would take the old piece
of cedar and go into the forest and stay there for four days
and the other spirits would come and share more words
and stories about great spirits who no longer existed
but you could see what they had created in their lives:
the rivers and mountains that were still here today.
And the new one would get up after four days and go back
into the world and could now speak the old language,
and the people would come to the new one asking for guidance,
so the new one would crumble the old piece of cedar
and tell the people that they must now suffer
so they can be cleansed of their wrongs and tell them
to leave the fish alone this year, let them all go home
and next year there would be more fish.
So the people would not fish and suffer from hunger
and the crumbling old cedar would hit the ground
and the rains would come and carry the dust
to the river to feed the fish as they all went home.

Dances in the Wind

On the river I throw my net out and watch it
drift down and soon there is a fish I take out
of the net and the wonder is clear: the mountains
melt and the trees dance and limbs look like limbs
dancing in a wind of sacred wind, like the Earth
sways each branch. A man or woman from the past
dances on the floor, their steps made but were also made
before. This dance is ours: we step and step and bow
our heads and we open our mouths. The song comes out
and everyone helps and the room is safe. We are the Kwantlen
and we are the ones who have survived as those before us
survived and danced and opened their mouths
as the words fall to the floor where footsteps shine.

The rains fall as the river slowly rises ...

and we are all joined together in some sort
of exception and we never know if this
is the day when we will all fall into the river
and yet we sit by the river and await the sun
as it becomes the fire in the sky for the day
and we await the moon who shyly comes over
the horizon of all of this and it is then we know
that it is time to venture into the water
and we all bathe the ugliness of ourselves away
and it gently floats out to the ocean and
there it is buried for the rest of our lives.

The snow fell and covered the earth
and we all began our walk up to the mountain
and there we sat down on the rocks
and knelt toward some god who had long ago
forsaken all of us but we pray anyway, we clasp
our hands together and some of us look up
into the sky but most of us look down
because we know we have failed this life
and that we owe so much to the sky
and as the snow falls we all become frozen
in a pose to a god we never knew.

The people gather in protest of something
or a purpose that explains why we are here
in the first place and it is the elders who are taken
away first and then the young who have no idea
as to why they are taken away and placed
somewhere other than on the land they have lived

on since time began and the elders weep
as they have seen this before and they raise
their hands into the air as if to say we are sorry.

In the village on an island there are those
who do not wish to live the good life
so vanish in their addictions and our people
again bury a child who was too young
to even begin to hate this place
and we bury them across the river
where they stay and there they weep
as they do not understand any of this
so we go back to our homes in our village
on that island where all of this began
and we close our doors and sit down
and weep for all the suffering of our people
as they yet again will wake up tomorrow
and some will kneel before a god they never knew
and the others will stand up and say enough
is enough as both the sun and the moon rise
as if confused as to the time of the day and
the rains shall fall as if they were our tears.

To Live with the Risen

We were always from this place
and will be here right to the end.
No one can tell us any different
so we gain the momentum
of a people who have lived before
and we sometimes look like we know
all the answers but never do
as life shells out its misery
so we laugh so much that our faces hurt
as we remember our past
as if it already happened.

There are those who came here
for all the wrong reasons
and they suffer the history of our people.
Some go so deep as to pity themselves
and we just laugh at them and tell them
to carry on the best they can—
They do, some of them, and when they return
they know a little more of the teachings
and accept their lives as we all do.

Every one hundred years a special child
is born to us and we welcome her
into our arms and cherish her life
and she cherishes ours and together
we watch as she becomes a simple healer
who heals those who have only been here
once before and in their weakness
she helps them live a good life—

They remember her and how she
touched them and they too
when they return
will be simple healers.

We all have returned for another go
at this and now we only number
just over two hundred and our young
look to us for some hope so we tell them
the old stories, how we remember them
and the children say thank you and we try
and try to provide a safe place for them
in this time where tragedy falls and the world
again is opposing us at every turn—
They take us again and try to change us
but our young who have lived before
say no and never again shall we fall off
this place we call ours and as the day ends
and a new child is born she looks to us
and touches us and heals us one more time.

The Constant Moment

Two ravens watch the woods
a songbird shakes her tail feathers
the constant moment here again
which of us deserves this
which of us deserved all that—
a gun is placed to temple
moved to the forehead
he settles in his kitchen
calls his family
phone dangles on the wall
screams of no
screams of why
the rifle straight
on the forehead
the trigger pulled
the explosion of death
the phone sits quiet
my grandfather slumps
blood and brain drips
this was when I was fourteen
this was my first death
ever since I am okay
the phone dangles
screams
silence
eternity.

Fish Stories

I liked the old stories
told by the old ones
that were so funny
that when they laughed
before the funny part
you knew you were gifted
in being allowed to listen—
always have your ears open
like that teaching
so simple
so divine.

One elder told us about
a fish who could smile
The fish smiled and the river
became full of fish
The fish smiled and the fish came to us—
We the Kwantlen have been here
since we fell from the sky
We were told we could take the fish
but today there are no more fish in the river
They do not smile
They do not dance
We are left here with funny stories
The past is the past
The future is the future
And we do not smile
We do not eat fish
No, we listen with ears open
to the last story.

How to Smoke a Dog Salmon

1

On the river with six hours to fish,
I throw my net out and watch it drift
past our old island. We have been here
forever and all our fires are burning.
It is a cold October morning and we are fishing
for dog salmon, big and thick and good for smoking.
My net begins to dance and the wind is cold
and the rain falls—I am soaked to the bone,
my hands are frozen and my eyes drip with rain.
I pull in my net and shake out the fish—
they fall to the floor of my boat,
then I throw them on ice. I fish the whole six hours
and my totes are full of dog salmon.
I bring my boat back around the inside
of our island, pull my fish and boat out of the river,
go home and clean all the fish,
taking their heads off first,
then slicing them up the belly
and pulling out the eggs and the guts.
I keep the eggs to sell later, cut the fish into strips
and salt and sugar them, then hang them up
in my smokehouse and wait a day.
I wait and then I light the fire—
the smoke goes up and I keep the fire going
for a few days. When they are done I take them down

and put them in bags. I sell some of them, and all the eggs,
but eat most of what I have caught over the long winter.
This is who we are, the Kwantlen,
the tireless people on an island in the river.

2

When the sun touches the moon
there is a story we tell our kids
of how not to get lost in the forest.
The kids sit and listen to an old storyteller
hanging on to every word spoken in our language.
They know their language,
we lost ours to schools and a book they called the bible—
it had some good stories but it all ended in hell.
We have our own hell.
The kids hide their eyes at the scary parts;
some shake and huddle together as the story ends,
then the kids run and play, they retell the story
and laugh in their language. The old storyteller goes back
to his home and sits by the fire another cold October day.
All the smokehouses are smoking the dog salmon,
the smell of fish and salt and sugar lingers
in the village, the village where we have lived
since time began. The kids are playing,
the fish is being smoked
as the storyteller closes his eyes
and dreams of smoked fish
to his lips: the salt and the sugar.

The Island

They told me I would never achieve more than what I had,
so I came here to this island and disappeared with the rest
of them. My family told me to leave and never come back
so I stayed, loved someone too close to me who lasted until
the pills came. My kids and I live in a small home on the edge
of the river where we laugh and cry and laugh and cry and
that is all. They told me to leave over and over and so inside
of me I left—the smoke rises from the ashes of a past
too horrid to share. We the people—survivors and fisherman
and the lovers who stayed. The river fills with fish and we set
our nets and watch the dance, clean the fish in the backyard
as the crows squawk and coo. The worms show up and robins
full-chested cut them to pieces. The cat sits with eyes closed
feeling the warm wind and the scents. There in the river
the fish swim home and we let them go and we wait—
The summer passes and the fall falls and the big dog salmon come
so we throw our nets and the winds change and the dogs
are caught and cut into strips and hung in the smokehouse
and days later taken down and chewed with beer. This is life
on an island where the people are small but tragic.

I open the book to page 333 and the story shifts:
I am inside, I am the book and the page is me, the arms
of deception fade, the once glorified writer weeps
his tears of loss and the pencil etches. There was talk
of greatness but I never saw any of it because of who I am
and the sins I have portrayed are the custom;
even if I were a little better with the words
someone would deny me, this is the life
of having pictures inside me and being all of me,

for every word that is shown is given a taste
of the blame and hate—you can call me liar a cheat
a non-hero and it would be close. So at the climax
of this story you will see inside of me and wonder—
The closing of the show is here and I am all alone
on an island and that is all they said I was.

The Day Begins

The rains finally fall and the smoke is gone
the day begins here on Reservation No. 6
where we grow slowly in numbers
each of us a burden to the other
and rumours abound let us look
at who we are and where we came
from our ancestors were small and strong
and they survived next up our young were taken
and told to love a god so we loved a god
who never really loved us back
then we drank and were not very good at it
even today we are not very good at it
then came addiction and self-pity and still we survived
today we have our past and our culture and it is enough
so we gather in the deep of winter and drum and sing
this is who we are and we are growing in numbers
the new ones have all that we have
they are strong and they stand up
and speak their tongue here on Reservation No. 6
an island
a place to live
even if you still drink the poison of our past.

Whispers in the Back of the Room

a people gathered to mutiny
we are one, are we?
or are we more than one
this begs us to answer
but no one does
we just sit in the back and whisper
as our Chief discusses money
and opportunity
we the people
the Kwantlen people
the tireless runners
the survivors of hate
we are one
or many
as the whisper
touches my ear.

The Climb

Even if we see the eagle
it is sometimes better to hear them.
They scream but it is such a lovely scream—
not a scream of hurt
but one of passion.
I sit outside and smoke and listen for them.
And they are there: two mates scream
to each other in their love
in their existence
in their survival.

When the river slows
and the rains fall heavy,
our boats are on the water
searching for the chum fish or dog salmon.
We sell the eggs, we smoke the meat.
I wait for my friend at the end of the road
to share a taste of smoked salted fish.
I take the rest home and bake the chunks
for a few minutes then throw on a pot of rice.
I feast and gorge myself as the dog looks at me
for a scrap; I give her a piece that she almost swallows
whole and we stare at each other and close our eyes:
we dream of the screaming in our heads.

Today I found out what has been ailing me
for the past year. I've been diagnosed,
have started the right medicines and have lost
near seventy pounds of fat and muscle.
I look old and weathered for fifty-six

but I am not going anywhere
as I have three kids to care and provide for.
So I begin the recovery of this old man.

The screaming ends and the rains stop.
The morning turns and the sun erupts
upon us all as we all heal in some way
or another. I eat an apple, then an orange
and then a banana and sip cold coffee
as I have yet to settle on a proper diet.
I still love steak and fish and all the foods
I should not be consuming. I suffer the gut pain
and survive the torment of proper eating.
The dog looks at me and reminds me
there is smoked fish in the fridge
from my friend down the road.
So I put on a pot of rice and bake it
for twenty minutes until the fat rises.
The dog and I go to my room to lay there
devouring our treat as the eagles love
each other, their scream for all of us.

The Man Who Was Once a Bear

A man was once a bear and he could climb trees
up there he felt at peace and he could see the world
if you are walking in the forest look up and you will see him
he likes the warm days the best and he scratches upon the branches
when he comes down he walks to the valley and finds berries
he eats until he pukes then eats some more
he was a man once and then was a bear and now he is a man
he does not climb trees and he does not care for berries
he eats fish and he likes to sit by the fire
he warms his old bones and he chews on smoked fish
his teeth are worn down and he has trouble seeing
he is old and his days of climbing trees are long gone
so he closes his eyes and he dreams of his woman
she was so small and she was never a bear
they loved each other and one day she left
he sits by the fire and he moans in his sleep
he misses her
he misses the trees
as the fire warms
this bear who was once a man.

Watch and Learn

Two eagles are fighting in the sky
a raven walks on the grass and pecks at death
wolves circle the kill and their eyes glow a mean yellow
under the water the fish are swimming back home
an old sasquatch sits by a fire and laughs
a young bear searches for fresh berries and a tree to scratch upon
the two eagles cry and cry and then tangle and fall
the raven opens its wings and is up into the blue sky
the wolves kill
the fish swim
the sasquatch laughs
the young bear sleeps in a cave
if you ever come across this please watch and learn
there are teachings for us all
never tangle with your lover
always fly to the blue sky
kill
swim
laugh
sleep the winter
remember the teachings.

Understanding the Dark Simplicity

The echoes of wisdom
do not reach me here on the river
I am on my boat and my net is drifting
I watch it closely and wait for it to dance
nothing hits it so I pull it in and go back upriver
I throw the net out again and drift
suddenly it begins to dance at the far end
I race over and begin to pull up the net
and there is a fifteen-pound spring
enough for supper and some to share
I put the fish on ice and go back to the end of my net
I pull it over closer to the middle of the river
there are snags where I am drifting
and I do not want to lose it
when I am past the danger I drift down farther
I begin to pull the net in
and there is another fish I did not see hit
a nice nine-pounder I will share with family
I call it a day and head back to our village
go home to clean my fish
then walk back down to the river
to throw the bones in they fall
feeding more of my family
those already gone to the other side
they feast on the bones
I feast on the fish
as the river decided
all of this.

The Dance

I am on my boat and throw
my net out and drift downriver
and watch to see if the net dances
and when it does I race over to pull it up
with a twelve-pound spring that I snap
out of the net and into my boat
then I let go, drift some more
then throw the fish into a tote with ice—
it still tries to swim but will soon be dead
and the net dances again, I pull out
a sixteen-pound fish and snap it out
of the net, throw it in with the other one
then once I've pulled all the net in
I point my boat back upriver and start
all over as the sun rises, the rains stop
and I light a cigarette and I am free.

The Rains Fall

After fifty days of sun
raindrops are warm
the fires up above us
smoulder and smoke
the sky is now dark
each of us knows the days
will now get shorter
and the nights longer
the seasons are changing
the fish should be here
but are so small in number
we do not feast
they tell us to wait
so we wait and when
they say go we go
our nets in the river
we can taste that first fish
as the rains fall
in a day or two
we will have enough fish
for the long winter
as the rains fall
we clean our fish
and put them away
the bones we give back
to the river
and we go home
we stir our fires
and cover up with a warm blanket
the river flows

and the fish we did not catch
swim home
where they bury their eggs
in the millions
four years from now
they will return
we will throw our nets
the rain will fall
the fires will rise
as once again we are given
the gift of repetition.

The Time of Ice

The gentle breeze of a December, all trees
stand motionless, we are the ones
who live here now on this island,
we are the ones who can see things
as they appear, we do not know all this
but we know if you see an owl
you should be careful, if you see
a black bird you should also be careful,
if you see a sasquatch you should
sit down and offer the sasquatch some fish
and if you are lucky enough the sasquatch
will share a story with you, and you should
share that story with your people.
Once a story was shared about a time
when there was ice and the river still flowed
full of fish and the moons were much brighter,
the sun was an angel, the trees did not move,
they stood, and the sasquatch ate the fish,
then stood up as the moon shone so bright.

Something in the Air

1

She could walk into a room
and no one would see her
The aroma of her entices all the men
and they look but she is gone
They try and kiss the air
hoping her lips are still there
She walks to the centre of the room
and begins to dance
All the men try to find her
to hold her one last time
She dances as the room
becomes full of smoke
and the men choke they fall
to the floor in anguish
as she raises her arms to the sky
She dances in a circle
and the men moan and begin to fade
The music is that of a soft drum
and voices sing an old song
The men are almost gone
except one who rises up
and finds her to embrace in dance
The room clears of smoke
They kiss as the last drum beats.

2

They fell in love on a street corner
held hands as they wept
tears of the past as both had suffered
but they had found love
in a room of smoke
When they kissed they knew
this was eternal love
this was how it should be
so they both kept the other alive
they shared everything
even the needle even the torment
in a room they huddled
watched the walls begin to move
the blood they shared became one
They could breathe together
in and out and in and out
They were one and suffered the love
outside in the street
The poor crept up the walls
The street people became bugs
that crawled on their skin
The lights went out
the room dark and cold
The two lovers huddled
screamed into the other's mouth
The bugs became butterflies
and danced on the walls
The room filled with smoke
as the butterflies erupted
Outside the street filled with smoke

Soon the earth was shade
Inside the room two lovers wept
They knew the end
The end was glorious
as the last butterfly burned.

Clarion Call

A cedar forest held all the wonders of the spirits;
they came from everywhere and sat in a circle.
A large bear spoke soft words in his language—
he spoke about the fish and how they were dying.
A small wolf spoke in her language and said
they were hungry. An old eagle spoke in his language
and said the river was empty when it should be full
of summer fish—most had not returned and those
that did were sick. The ocean was also dying
and all the fish with it. A young coyote spoke
in his language and said he was hungry.
When all had spoken, they all began
to sing the spirit song. It could be heard
across the river, but the ocean could not hear it—
the ocean died and the world died,
as it spoke in its language.

Poetic Inspiration

The books pile up on my desk.
I have read them all and most
were not worth the effort. I dragged
my eyes across the words and now they sit
in a row or on a pile—some of the art
on the covers is nice but the words inside
do not urge me to want to ever read again.

So I must tell the writers that their work hit me,
even though it never did. I wish I could be
more honest but I just want to keep writing
in peace without the drama of telling them
that they really need to live more
but most are spoiled and have been given it all.
I want to tell them to read my books
and see the pain and anguish of a man
who lived on the streets
who drank many a bottle
who loved and lost
who spent many a day in madhouses
and the quiet white rooms of many a hospital
where he found the meaning
of this one
and that one
and, of course, that one.

My Glasses Are Dirty

Vivaldi spins in the back of this room where I come every morn
to write poems so I can pay the bills and feed my kids.
And so the words leave the mind and become a sort of story
that goes like this. When all is said and done, I will have filled a room
full of unwanted poems. I sneeze and that feels wonderful
and I feel another sneeze coming but it fades, and the violins echo
off the mountains and I am at peace with all of this and write a poem
for all of you as you open this book and imagine the screaming orchestra
as she weeps a sweet melody for the folks across the river
where they bury a loved one in the dirt of all our souls.

I stare down and am not sure why I do, so I lift my head up
and tell the world that I am still here in this shit and memory
of who I was and who I could have been, and I light a smoke
and inhale and exhale and the dogs run in circles as the birds
chase dreams that fell away a long time before I looked down
and now I look up to the sky where more birds circle the world
and they begin to sing an opera of war and shame and the other
birds sit in trees and they are the audience of this shame and
this story is about the war the birds had with some coyotes
who ate their young and how the birds had massed into a ball
of attack and the coyotes ran away to the river and they dove
in as the birds attacked and it was a good battle and the war
was over as the violins screamed.

They told me I was manic and depressed and violent,
and they told me to see a doctor so I did, and he did not care
too much for me—he told me so and he laughed at me
and prescribed me the right meds and the wrong diagnoses
for my mind but when I left his office, I heard him tell the nurse

that I would never be back and that one day I would either be dead
or in jail and I proved him wrong but the meds worked and I slept
at night and I was no longer violent and now I smoke way too much,
and I no longer have dreams of killing my ex and she went
her own way and left me with the kids and we actually became good friends,
but she perished in a ball of pills and on that day, I had to tell my kids
that their mom had gone and they screamed at me and I tried my best
to be calm and not manic but that doctor was right and I never went back.

The Parade

We all were given one pair of cotton slippers as the floor
of this hospital is quite cool and most of the men here
have already lost one of their slippers so there is a parade
of men with droopy eyes and one slipper and they walk
around the rooms and drool as the meds here are strong
and I sit by the window and look out to see all the cars go
by as the hospital is near the highway which is good
as when they bring someone new here, the access
from the city is easy, and they always show up
with sirens blaring and tires squealing
and open the door as if the man they're bringing in
is so in need of saving but we all are, yes,
we all are worth saving in one way or another
and I look out the window at a small bird sitting
on a tree branch thinking I have been here only a week
and want to go home to sit by my own window
and stare at the people as they walk by in their desire
to survive and when the bird on the tree flies away
I turn and look at the parade as it crashes to an end,
the men all slipping on the newly washed floor
and most lose the other slipper joining those
who go barefoot in another parade, which I will soon
join as I am one slipper down, one slipper on.

When it's suppertime, we all line up and take a tray
and a plastic spoon and tonight it is soup and a piece
of dried toast and a plastic cup of apple juice
and I sit alone, and they leave me alone
as I have already beaten two of these men who thought
I was a target and tried to steal my one slipper

so I dropped the first one with a punch to guts
and the second came from behind me and knocked
me down but I got up and planted my bare foot kicking
him in the head and my one slipper flew off.
I will join the parade later so sit alone and no one
bothers me and some men even give me their apple juice
as I had beaten the bullies of this place
where the floor is quite cool.

I talk to a doctor once a week and she always says
the same thing, telling me to stay a while longer
and the meds will help so I stay, and I become the man
with those around me giving me cigarettes and I will fix
any problem or person for them and soon I've been there
for six months when the doctor finally says I should go
home now and that they've become concerned
that even the nurses fear me, and know I have a racket
of selling pills given to me from men who need my help.
So the next day I am given a pair of shoes and put them on,
and they feel so different I shuffle more than step,
as they open the door for me and I walk out into the garden
and there the birds have gathered, and I say hello
and they take off and I walk toward the highway
just as they bring in someone new who looks droopy
and drools and swears he was the second coming
and I think about the parade he will soon be joining
with all the gods of the place walking and talking
the truth, as if the truth mattered.

This Last Century

I rise up each morning and go out the door
and begin the same day again and again.
I am at peace with this; I start my truck
and away I go to the next step and the next.
The day resembles me: how I am,
how I could be, but I just stay the same
and light a smoke and sip a hot coffee
and blow the smoke out the window
and crank up the heat and crank up
a good tune on the radio and my truck tires
splash last night's rain. I pull into my office
and rearrange three painted skulls on my desk.
I have repeated this as part of the routine
and I light some medicine. It burns,
the smoke is my saviour. I begin to type
as the words fall. I was not a very good drunk—
if you could name someone who was,
I would like to meet them—but for me
I would get drunk and then fight and wake up
stinking in a cell in the local drunk tank.
I could not remember any of it, all I knew
was my knuckles were torn, I had scraped
my knees and my head hurt with a few welts.
When they called my name and let me go home
I would walk out into the morning to the bus
and travel the hour home and open the door,
take off all my stinking clothes,
take a hot shower, get dressed for work
and go out the door. I would wonder where
the weekend had gone, would work hard

all week and forget all the pain.
When Friday came, they would give me
my cheque and out the door I'd go
to the bar to drink my first beer.
In the corner a man would be staring at me
like he knew me but did not like me
and as the night went on, the drinks would flow
and that man would approach me outside
and that is all I could remember.

We would smoke hash and weed, we took acid,
snorted speed, we washed it down
with a mickey of rye. I was only fifteen
and had not lived much but I was a good friend
if I needed to be and so we all would meet
in the woods and shared what we had, smoked
and drank and then a girl would come up to me
and we would go deeper into the woods
or to her house or my room
where we would make love—
we were so wasted—she would take me
and I would take her, and this went on all summer,
and then I met a girl I fell in love with
off and on for next twelve years
until I drove away and fell in love with
another girl who I thought loved me
but actually loved another so I smashed him
and got in my old car and headed west
where I have been for the last twenty-five years
and where I have loved and hated, have been loved
and hated and do not drink or do drugs,
no, I write bad poems to recall the pain in me.

The Day Ends Early

An eagle sits on our tallest tree—
I whistle to it and I raise up my hands
but get nothing from the eagle so finish
my smoke and sit down and burn
some sage and ask for good thoughts
for my family, friends and children
and then begin to type a poem about me
it is always about me, do not be fooled
if you think I could write about
anyone else, I do not really know
anyone else, how they have lived,
how they have lasted this long
or even how I have lasted this long
outside I hear the eagle screaming at me
as she glides over my office and spreads
her wings, waiting for an answer
that never comes. A death has entered
our village and the family does the best
they can to care for their loved one
as the village weeps and the rains begin
to fall as day begins, but it is still dark
outside, and the day ends early—
it is again dark out, the family can
only meet for a short time, there is
a sickness in the world, we are all
close to dying, so we close our village
as we have already survived smallpox
which wiped out 80 percent of us and now
we are only a scattering of over two hundred
and the family of the lost one gather to spread

the ashes and sing old songs, they are all gifted
with old songs and old words and we sit here
in our self-isolation as the rest of the world learns
how to perish without medicine and glory.

The Writing Life

I ready some envelopes to send my books
out to those who wish to have them.
I've never been good at being a writer
so I sign each book as if I am famous
to make me feel somewhat important,
then sit in my office sipping a double-double
with a shot of expresso, the sun shining.
When I'm done writing a poem to share
in my next book, I close my notebook
and change the song on the radio
as some band tells me I am ahead by a century.

Virtuoso

I am on a stage reading some poems
I give them my best and after that it does not matter
it does not matter if I am any good at this
I take their money and I thank them for asking me to share
I walk the sidewalk and get in my truck
the drive is quiet and I play music softly
the road takes me across a big bridge
I look over the edge and I can see the river
it flows to the east and out to the ocean and it becomes salty
I make it home and I can still hear the applause
they loved me and my poems
they cried a few tears and laughed when I told them to
I read some old poems and some new ones
they loved them both and they clapped for me
for me this old poet from upriver
I make it to my bed
I lay down and stare at the money they had given me
I wonder what I will buy with it as I close my eyes
the peacefulness of this becomes another poem
to be shared later
and for
much
much
more
money.

Sands of Time

There are days like today when the pain
and loss overcome me and I sit here smoking
way too many smokes and replaying tunes
that keep me afloat. And the blood falls
from my eyes and puddles upon an old dead leaf
that fell weeks ago and now dances around
the building where I hide myself from a world
that would take one look at me and be overcome
by the desire to put me away in a soft place
I've been to a few times—where someone changes
my meds when they are not working.

The blood drips and falls on another dead leaf—
this one still has some life, it dances across
the gravel road and ends up tangled in
a blackberry bush where the thorns prick it
and if you could just walk over to me
and give me a hug and some kind words,
tell me I look okay when I do not look okay
because I have lost over one hundred pounds
and my skin hangs over the edges of who I used to be;
I smoke more and fade even more as the blood
drips again, but this time there is no leaf,
as the other leaves have fallen last week
and the emptiness of me is the emptiness of me.

I sip some water and change the song on the radio
where the singer pleads with us not to judge him
because he has no idea if he belongs here
and I do not belong here; I should be on

the warm sands by the ocean south of here,
only a plane ride away, but I settle in for
the winter and all that comes with it—
the sorrow falling from the mountains,
another winter but different: no gathering
this year to help someone who needs help,
so we all sing to ourselves as we walk around
the room imagining what it should look like.

I sip some water and dream
about what I should be doing but the sands
are warm so I walk into that ocean and dive
down, taste the ocean and hear an airplane
passing overhead: I am in seat 29C
sitting beside an angel of a woman
who has escaped as well—we meet on the sands
for dinner where she laughs at me, I laugh at me,
and she tells me she is there to discover who
she is supposed to be, and I tell her
perhaps it was to meet me, and that
we should finish our dinner and walk the sands.

She agrees: we laugh some more, then go
to her room where she tells me to sit
on the bed, she will be right back.
So I sit on the bed and listen to the ocean,
an airplane flying overhead…
She walks in naked, comes to me
and we kiss, pushes me back on the bed,
the sands of this time are true and real.

Kind Words

You will miss me as the sun sets and the day
becomes night and all of it fits so nicely together
when you think about it and we do think about it
too much and that is why we waste so much of it
on the day-to-day shit that we worry about
and if we could just take a second and erase
the last thirty years we could move on as the sun
sets and the night comes and we could use our dreams
as beacons for where we have not walked
and if we try too hard we always get to the same
spot in our minds that dwells way too much upon
the hurt and the lies and the loss of trust we had
for each other and that is what love is for all of us
as we pick ourselves up from the floor and we try
again to fall in love but it is never the same
and you can taste it on your tongue as you smell
the air around you and you kiss the dreams away
and every night when you are all alone you cry
yourself to sleep and when you wake up the next
morning and it all tastes the same you get up
and you kiss the air just to make sure.

Freedom is all I could think of when I was
put away in a brightly lit home where they fed us
pancakes for breakfast and steak for dinner
but most of us were too sick to chew so we sipped
the broth and we tried a piece of dried toast
and then we all went out to the pretty garden
and smoked until our fingers turned yellow
and stained and then we went in for our morning

meds and I swallowed mine as if they were candy-
coated gems and then we were given time to reflect
upon our deeds and our wishes as the day shift came
on board and they were either too young to be there
or they were too old and had been there too long
and they would just kick us into the backroom
where there were puzzles with missing pieces
and the truly mad just sat on the floor and scratched
their fingernails to the bone and rocked back and forth
as if in prayer but for me it was the time that I went in
and allowed the meds to take me to a place so peaceful
that I was out of there in three weeks and I had fooled them
again and out to the streets I went and I fell to the ground
and I rocked back and forth as if in prayer.

The drugs were good when I was a teenager
but I did not know about the effects it would
have on me when I was much older but we
did them anyway and I would slip into
a deep high on LSD and for twelve hours
I would see the deepest colours and the walls
caved in and I would swim away into an ocean
of calm and we would drink the whole time
we were high and when the high faded
we were so drunk we just stared at each other
and sometimes I'd be with a girl and we'd
make love as the sun came up. I was so good
at all this that when I finally quit at twenty-six
I realized how much of my life I'd wasted
and would not waste anymore on shit and booze
and drugs so that was when I went back to school
and remembered what a book was; it was then

that I cut out my first poem and now the poems
come every day—I can sit here for hours and watch
the colours change as I swim in an ocean of discovery.

Nine a.m. and I have been up for six hours.
I have already accomplished most of what
I had planned out but there is still so much
to do and I have to rework some old poems
and I have to catch up on letters and pieces
of art that are incomplete and there is my old boat
which needs some love and care and the lawn is due
for a cut but the rains fall and it can wait—
also I have to get more dog food and need more movies
to watch at night and perhaps a book or two to read
while I await the next morning and there is always
the kids to feed and to listen to and to make sure
they are doing okay as we are all so anxious
and concerned about the world and the sickness
upon us and they too are afraid of getting sick
and I am worried for them as well but we have
made it through and our people were sick
a long time ago and smallpox wiped us out
but we still survive after ten thousand years
and here I sit reworking old poems
that never worked in the first place.

Men from upriver sing and drum songs of prayer
as we go and set our nets and we tell those men
to stop praying because we have filled our nets
and the fish are here and they keep singing
and the fish come and we all laugh and joke
as we pick the hundreds of fish from our nets

and then they feed us and bring us water
and coffee and we light a smoke and sit
and wait for the next boat to come in
and people from upriver come and fill their buckets
and there is no time to sing and so we pick fish
and laugh and joke and tease one of our own
and she laughs and takes the jokes and then turns
on someone else and then we all turn on that person
and we pick the hundreds of fish from the net
and that is the end of the day as we have caught
enough and tomorrow we will drum and sing
and pray and throw our nets out and it will appear
like a new day as the laughter falls to the river
where all of this belongs.

First and Last Impressions

1

The touch of her was enough
to allow me the much-needed love
we had met in a faraway land no one knew about
she told me I was her first, I told her the same
we were fourteen, both of us skinny and brown
she had dark eyes and long black hair
I had deep brown eyes and long black hair
we were from different reservations
but we spoke the same tongue
we were drunk on a Friday night
and all our friends had left—
it was just me and her and she accepted me and I entered
she moaned that it hurt but to keep going
so I kept going and she kept moaning
I could not hold on any longer and we both cried out
we stayed there on floor of her bedroom and laughed
we laughed at how clumsy we had been
she told me I was her first
I told her she was my first
decades later we met at a poetry reading
I recognized her right away
it was the dark eyes
and she told me
I was her first.

2

We met on an eastern reservation in the dead of winter
she was so beautiful and I was the same
we both loved the winter and she loved my words
we were lovers for one winter and one spring
I knew I could not keep her and she made this very clear
so I loved her as much as she allowed me to
we laughed and we loved music and she had a baby
and he was near us when we made love, the three of us
a sort of lover's family for a winter and part of a spring
I still write to tell her I love her
we both now have kids of our own
she tells me about hers and I tell her about mine
one winter decades ago on an eastern reservation
as the snow fell and melted and the one spring
opened the door for me, I went out and never went back
those lover's hours spent near a child given to us for eternity.

We met on our Reservation No. 6 beneath the mountains
beside the river near the cool waters of small streams
she took me for hers and she would not let go
I tried to leave but she would stand in my way
I tried to run but she would hold me tight
we were lovers for fifteen years and we had three kids
I am with them now as she passed two years ago
we found her on the floor, they did all they could to save her
my kids and our village helped her to get to the other side
there she would make them laugh and cry
here we laugh and cry and remember her as funny and tough
she says goodbye and we burn her favourite foods for her
the smoke rises and her kids all laugh
they remember her for her laughter
as the smoke falls she appears before us
smiles that wicked smile, turns and she is gone
her and the smoke fade
as the river stops
starts
carries on.

Wipe Out Those Who Sink

Ever since I can remember I was always ugly
I saw myself in every mirror: eyes beautiful
nose crooked but acceptable
ears firm and tucked in
lips kissable and luscious
eyelashes were wanted
my one eyebrow a gift from my old man
my teeth crooked and weak
my chin soft and filled with glass
my cheeks were mine.

The days have brought me out
of this smug laughter, steps taken
one at a time, almost a sad shuffle
laughter in the house and the kids
are on their way, all the dogs
are barking and biting and chewing
the cat sleeps and dreams
of fresh rats and rabbits.
Outside the smoke floats
as the cigarette burns to filter
my feet ache and I took off
one toenail moving a heavy desk
it no longer bleeds but is sore
and it too aches with a smile—
The day is hot and the sun
is glamorous and the birds sing;
there is a dream of a better place
than this old reservation
the river rises as if it could never stop

and it flows forever
mosquitoes show themselves
and their bloodthirsty minds
the dogs bark and the cat meows
and the birds sing as rain appears
the night comes and I am outside
burning a smoke and dying—

You see this is who I am
I think, yes, I am the lonely man
the lonely man who lies in bed
alone beside his old dog
the emptiness of self-pity exits
out the window as the candle burns
another day in the life of a forgotten poet
who writes to his end.

This is the end and there was
a beginning and a middle—
those were good times
and drunken times and laughing times,
there was love and she knows
who she is and there were children
and now they move on
and out to the world—I hope
I have given them enough
to seek a better way of living
except I made many mistakes
and it was the yelling and the anger
a memory of my childhood
as my old man threw me around.
His love, so he said, was pure

for me but we know the abuser,
we know the hate of life
by those who hated life
and we loved them.

The end is around the corner
as the city erupts into a dark film
the stars of the film fall to the ground
and the camera follows me—
it follows me to my room
and the bed where the old dog sleeps;
the outside moon lights up
the forgotten and the lost and we weep.
Yes, let those tears fall for me
as this is the end and the end
is so pure, the tug of the trigger
on a gun with one bullet
stolen from a friend.
It hits me and I become
a memory and in a book
where they will call me insane.

Top of the Mountain

My only regrets and broken thoughts
are for me to take with me
when I go to the mountain
to sit down one more time
and gaze at the Earth and a place
where I have been chosen to live and die.

I take with me my nightmares
and grief and with a final breath
I exhale the putrid mind given to me
when I was about five and fell
from a high stairway and cracked my head
and my mother came running out
of the house to hold me
as the doctors told her I was okay
but later in life when I placed the gun
to my head and thoughts of why
I am here pounded inside me
I could not see a future
but only the lost love of a girl
who did not love me the same.
And when they found me
on the mountain they took me back
and I sat in that cold room
with walls painted so white and pure.
I rocked back and forth and
they said the medicine would help.
It did, and I came out of there
with a new mind and the gun
sits quietly on the top of a mountain.

The Ancient Spoils

In the morning today I took out six bags
of garbage and left them by the side of the road.
In them were the spoils of me and my kids
and the dogs and the cat and I prayed
the black birds would not come and pick at the bags
because the garbage man will not take bags
with holes in them. The sun came up, I had slept in
and was to go to the city to meet a girl and gift her
copies of my bad poetry at a coffee shop.
I thought about taking a shower but decided to go
as I am, with clothes I had been wearing
and sleeping in for a week and the smell of tobacco
and the dog sleeping beside me every night.
The sun lit the morning, and down the road
a friend of mine was smoking fish,
and I thought I could let the smoke cover me
and meet the girl smelling of smoked fish,
how ancient I would be, how my books
of weak poetry would be given to her as a gift,
then I would drive out of the city, home to
the garbage gone, black birds nowhere in sight,
smoke and the smells of the ancient float.

I Am the Wanted

Whispers come from a corner of the room
and there she sits as she has always sat.
I look into her eyes and she tells me
I have done good, I should move on
so I do, I move on, and when I look
in the corner, she is gone as if never there
in the first place and when I go out to the world
where I shall be the most wanted man
I walk with such pureness the women come to me
wishing to dance, so we dance in a circle.
They all want me—I have to choose just one
to stay with for the rest of my life and I choose
a young poet of a girl, so quiet and sweet,
and we dance until the sun comes up,
then go to my room where in the corner
my lover weeps as if wanted.

So the river is low, the rains fall,
the smoke from wood stoves
goes up into the moist air.
In each house there is one or two of us
and we have been here a long time
so the books tell us we are the ones
who have survived yet another sickness—
it is like this all along the river
and each people has those
who have survived, they are now
sitting in their home placing wood
into their stoves as the winter rains fall
the river is low, and the boats

are all tied up for a few months
until the spring fish come home
there are moments like this one
where time is all we want.

The Sting Kills

I crack my knuckles more these days,
sometimes several times, and I think I like the feeling—
certainly like the noise but it has become as boring
as most of the tics I have created, so I stop
and move on to the next one: I pick out one hair
from my eyebrow and stare at it, this too bores me
as there is no sound from it. When I smoke, I breathe in
as fast as I can. This bores me so I stop and inhale slower,
enjoying the poison, then I go to the world and drive my car,
same radio station giving me rock 'n' roll from the past
and even that is boring, so I flip the station and now
it is playing classical music old as time, and the sound
gives me reason as if I ever needed one.

Through the Panes

1

A shadow follows me and there is one of me
it looks kind we all are followed by something
we know it well but I seem to not be able
to accept it and there it stands all along a wall of stones
they had found me passed out on the church's steps
praying and puking and dying and then the sirens
the doctor told me to stop drinking I did not listen
as soon as I was out I went to the corner store
left with a bottle then stooped in a doorway
I sipped and sipped my friends had all left
I was alone in the night of dreams
I slept for a few hours
then awoke with such a headache
my eyes watering my belly burning
I got another bottle this would be my last
I went to the church to sleep
they found me crucified by my own shadow
painted on the wall of stones
a monument to a forgotten man
him his shadow wept.

2

The flash of the pipe and I am lit up ready to run
five dollars' worth of rock burnt to the bare glass
the street is full of mean folks and their victims
the working girls and boys line up to get their taste
then run away and play in the background
next the old addicts line up and scrounge for change
they walk away some float up to the beginning of night
next it is me and the other thieves we trade our trinkets
I get my piece of the mountain and light it up
the breath of dust enters my brain and I am flying
I go deeper into the city rob the rich smoke the poor
I nearly get caught but am still a tireless runner
they stop chasing me I am back in line as the old ones float
it is my turn the devil hands me some rocks
I trade beads stolen from a diamond store and the Devil
is handed thirty pieces the gold in his hands turns to flames
as the working kids dance and dance the night has just begun
as we all join the drugged dance of addiction
each of us so elegant each of us so fucked up
as the Devil deceives us just like he did in a book
in a time of deception.

3

The words of who I am are simple and precise
I am a loner and I am lost in my own mind this is me
carefully I can accept all this and move forward with ease
but there are times I cannot move and cannot breathe
so I stop and wait for the moment to pass then breathe
it is inside me that's the trouble I try to walk the walk
even on nights when I'm all alone in a big bed with a blanket
I cover up and the fan blows warm air in the dead of summer
I cover up and close my eyes and there I can see all of me
washing up on the shores of an ocean as the seabirds scream
I come out of the water naked and cleansed this is who I am
the mind I have cannot have me forever so I walk the shores
to find rocks and flowers but there are none so I keep walking
when I awake in my big bed the blanket is gone and the fan blows
I get up and look in the cracked mirror trying to see me
but the image is someone else—he looks at me and smiles.

4

Today I am quite normal and in control of my mind
I smoke and drink coffee and that is the extent of it
I no longer have violence as a vice and my hands have healed
my face not so lucky the scars and the crookedness are mine
when I look in the mirror I can just make out the beauty
in my eyes they are still a soft brown though one is higher
than the other they tried to sew me up as best they could
when those two men kicked in my face and I am now
very crooked but my eyes are there and I can look into them
trying to see the past but my mind won't let me so I look forward
and that is much better and then I smoke and I drink coffee
as the mirror is shaded—it is me, I think.

5

There were times when I would sit on a bus and look out
trying to see what there was for me here and at this time
she had left me years ago and we were no longer in touch
I tried to reach out but she was gone and I was on a bus
the city was cold and the day was bright with a cold sun
she was gone and I was gone and so I wrote poems for her
the books of poetry were bad and sullen and full of self-pity
you may find one in the garbage or an old bookstore
check out the section of broken-heart crap
my books are there on the shelf beside the greats
take one home and read it on the toilet and see the pain
each line a cut into me as she deceived me and she was right—
you see I could never love and she knew that
she made the right choice and I am still here
looking out the window as the world freezes.

A Writer's Nightmare

Red

I am known as a red-faced man
made by those who were black, brown and red
so I dance
to the corners of any room
as the drums pound my song.
I bless the floor
as the floor
turns red.

Glass

I am the broken glass thrown at me by my mother
because I would not eat Kraft Dinner.
I was reminded every day by the imprint it had made
in the wall behind my head. Poor Mom—
those nuns and priests destroyed her so long ago
when the children were starved
and a bowl of macaroni would have saved some of them.

River

I am the river.
I was born underneath,
then one day I was asked to become a man.
They found me some clothes to wear
and they did not fit, I looked quite funny
but they said it would be okay
so I walked out of the river

and the river kept going and when I became a man
they told me to wait by the river
so I have been here for thousands of years
waiting and waiting.
My clothes now fit
and I am quite the man
if I ever knew
what a man was.

Self-pity

It is what we are taught in our spiritual ways—
that we are not to pity ourselves—
and it is a hard one, that one. When you are tired
and broken, how can you not pity yourself?
You do and so does everyone else.
And I am pity.
I am the self.
As the days mask the truth of me
and the days mask the truth of me
as I am pity,
I am pitiful
as outside of me the others begin to pity themselves
and the spirits see this: they laugh at us
as we are now full of sorrow:
we are the sorrow,
we are the teardrop,
we are in pain
as our backs and legs ache
with the weight of carrying around all this sorrow.
But the spirits laugh as they, too, pity themselves.
Yes, even the spirits are full of pity:

they are the pity
and I am selfish
as I fall to my knees
begging for pity—
I am the pity.

Count the Days

To lose in life is to lose in life and so I count the days that are left. You cherish the good and spit out the bad and keep the sacred. The old ones told of a day like this one where all would fall into place, so I count the days and here I am in this one and I am okay with that, the sun is up and the sky is blue and the birds sing; they are happy with all the worms they can eat and share. The sun rises over the mountains and shines its rays of hope. To lose is to lose and we all have lost someone close to us—we bury ours across the river in an old graveyard. We keep it clean and we are ready for the next one: it could be me and it could be you, it depends on how many days like this one we have left. So we walk in the sun and we hear the birds. I count this day as one of many. I hope I can count for a long time, but you never know, you never know the loss of a day.

The Moon Shine Shades Black Clouds

Look for your love in the rooms along the street
littered with the lost who vow to never leave
this utopia called *the east* and if you do find your love,
make sure you make love when the moon shine shades
the black clouds and if it is cloudless imagine
the clouds as they form in a circle above your bed
where you and your lover entwine in a dance so old
that even the violins cannot keep up with all of this lust
and when you are done light a cigarette and pass it to her
and admire her naked beauty as she talks about her family
and how they still live outside of this *east*
and the moon shine shades the black clouds.

The colour of deception is right there beside me
as I walk out of the store where I bought a Coke
and some smokes for a quarter each and I go stand
on the corner and the masses pass me by and some look
and some smile but most are so lost in their deep desire
to score a piece of white rock that they do not see me
at all and I stand there until later in the morning
and then make my way up the block and get in line
for a sandwich, a piece of pie and some hot black coffee.
I sit down and listen to the word of God and the speaker
is a wino who changed his mind about dying
in the blood of Christ so he quit drinking and now stands
before us as we chew quietly on cheese sandwiches
and sip hot black coffee. As I listen to this ex-wino
I notice a woman who sits at the front and she is swaying
from side to side chanting as the wino tells us about
the birth of Christ as it is a week to Christmas,

which is the hardest time for us street folk,
and as he finishes the woman who was chanting
begins to float above the room and she floats out the door
as the cheese sandwiches are chewed quietly.

I had seen them float before—usually it was from one street
to another—and they always had their arms out as if flying
like a bird but none of them looked like a bird, no,
they were all shattered and broken and they closed their eyes
as they floated to the ground and landed quite well
and they would walk onwards, and some stayed in the air
for some time but most fell and then more would
take to the sky and through all this I was standing again
on that corner eating a candy bar and when I was done,
I would light a smoke and beside me a woman landed feet-
first and she stood beside me for hours and we both watched
the masses as they bounced along the sidewalk.

Then she turned to me and we fell in love
and went back to my room. I cleaned the papers
from the bed and took her—and she let me,
and she began to chant and sway from side to side
and just then the wino appeared outside the window
but he did not look in as he floated up and never came
down as the woman chanted and I closed my eyes
as the moon shades the black clouds of eternity.

The Cheerfulness of Nothing Else

She weeps so softly
we talked about old times
I mentioned school
she breathed in and a tear fell
from her eye I tried to move on
she breathed in and stared at me
for a long time I did not breathe
and hoped her mind would change
she breathed in and then laughed
at the cat which she hated
the window was not open
it was beyond hot in her room
she tried to get up for some tissue
as I watched her every step
she made it back and sat down
as if upon a throne
though her chair was an old chair
she sat straight and proud
if she had a crown it would
of course be of thorns.

for me this son of a great woman
who now has Parkinson's
they said she is doing well
after breaking both her hips
she wept today as I write
the words break the skin
there is no one here for me
though my children keep me well
for them I write and steal a scene

or two from my mom
her memory clouded
but still there and still full of scenes for me
I like the one about how she
has no smell and no sense of direction
she laughs and the window is open
and the warm air is all she has
she wears a woollen hat
even in the dread of summer
her socks too big for
feet washed by God
this will one day be
in one of my poems
as the window closes.

There used to be a hanging tree
that we all knew about
they say it was from the old school
that my mother went to
where she was abused
and used and tossed away
she did not conform to
the world they said was better
she kept her spirit inside
of her for fifty years
now she walks slow
and her mind walks slow
she is still that little girl
taken on a train at five years old
told to forget
now she forgets
her mind soiled by disease

she keeps the bible close
turned to a page of existence
the father and the son
watch over her
she cannot kneel anymore
her hips broken
her mouth waters
she is my mother
and she is
my mother.

About the Author

Joseph Dandurand is a member of the Kwantlen First Nation, located on the Fraser River about twenty minutes east of Vancouver, BC. He resides there with his three children. Dandurand is the director of the Kwantlen Cultural Centre and the author of several books of poetry including *The East Side of It All* (Nightwood Editions, 2020), which was shortlisted for the Griffin Poetry Prize. In 2021, Dandurand received the BC Lieutenant Governor's Award for Literary Excellence.